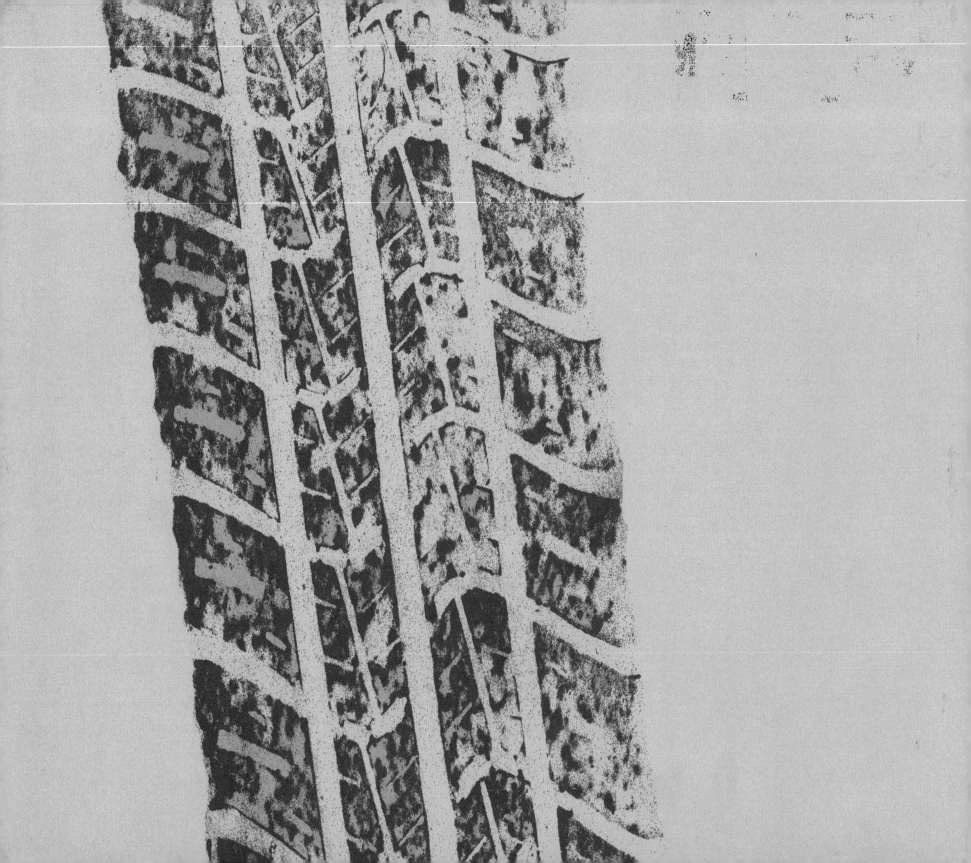

I DRIVE A GARBAGE TRUCK

by Sarah Bridges

illustrated by Derrick Alderman & Denise Shea

PICTURE WINDOW BOOKS
Minneapolis, Minnesota

Thanks to the Twin Cities Waste Management team—S.B.

Thanks to our advisers for their expertise, research, and advice:

Joe Gray, Gray Sanitation

Manson, Iowa

Susan Kesselring, M.A., Literacy Educator

Rosemount-Apple Valley-Eagan (Minnesota) School District

Managing Editors: Bob Temple, Catherine Neitge
Creative Director: Terri Foley
Editors: Brenda Haugen, Christianne Jones
Editorial Adviser: Andrea Cascardi
Designer: Nathan Gassman
Storyboard development: Amy Bailey Muehlenhardt
Page production: Banta Digital Group
The illustrations in this book were rendered digitally.

Picture Window Books
5115 Excelsior Boulevard
Suite 232
Minneapolis, MN 55416
877-845-8392
www.picturewindowbooks.com

Library of Congress Cataloging-in-Publication Data
Bridges, Sarah.
I drive a garbage truck / by Sarah Bridges ; illustrated by
   Derrick Alderman and Denise Shea.
p. cm. — (Working wheels)
Includes bibliographical references and index.
ISBN 1-4048-0615-6 (reinforced library binding : alk. paper)
1. Refuse collection vehicles—Juvenile literature. 2. Refuse
   collectors—Juvenile literature. 3. Refuse and refuse
   disposal—Juvenile literature. [1. Refuse and refuse disposal.
   2. Trucks.] I. Alderman, Derrick, ill. II. Shea, Denise, ill.
   III. Title. IV. Series.
TD794.B73 2004
628.4'42—dc22   2003028227

3

4

My name is Jackie, and I drive a garbage truck.

While I'm driving, my partner rides on back of the truck.

A driver checks the truck's brakes, tires, and fluids before driving.

We wear special clothes to do our job. Gloves protect our hands. Bright vests help other drivers see us when it's dark. Boots keep our feet from getting **wet** or **cold.**

The special gloves garbage collectors wear are made of tough leather. They protect their hands from sharp items like glass.

8

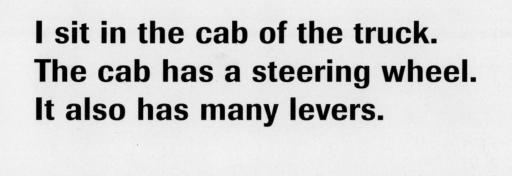

I sit in the cab of the truck.
The cab has a steering wheel.
It also has many levers.

Some garbage trucks have a camera on the back of the truck. The camera helps the driver see what's behind the truck.

My partner collects the garbage. He empties it into the back of the truck.

My truck has mirrors that help me see what my partner is doing.

Some garbage trucks only need one person.
The driver controls an automatic arm.
The arm picks up and empties garbage
cans into the truck.

My partner and I pick up a lot of garbage. Every day we have a different route. We visit about 350 houses on each route!

Garbage collectors can often tell how many people live in a house by how much garbage they produce.

We collect lots of *different* kinds of trash.

We don't pick up things that can be recycled.
The recycling truck picks up cans, glass,
paper, and plastic.

Things that are recycled are turned
into new things and reused. Recycling
cuts down on waste.

15

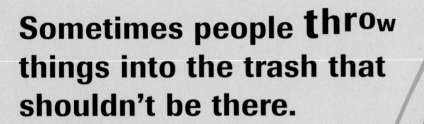

Sometimes people **thro**w things into the trash that shouldn't be there.

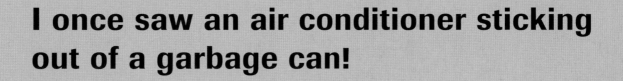

I once saw an air conditioner sticking out of a garbage can!

Things such as air conditioners, refrigerators, and computers can't be thrown out with regular garbage. Some cities have special cleanup days each year when these things can be disposed of or recycled safely.

When the truck is full, I drive to the landfill or incinerator. That's where I empty out the trash. Then the garbage is either **buried** or *burned*.

The garbage truck visits the landfill or incinerator several times each day to empty the garbage.

When we're done,
I drive the truck back to
the garage for the night.

After we wash the truck,
it is ready for another
trip tomorrow.

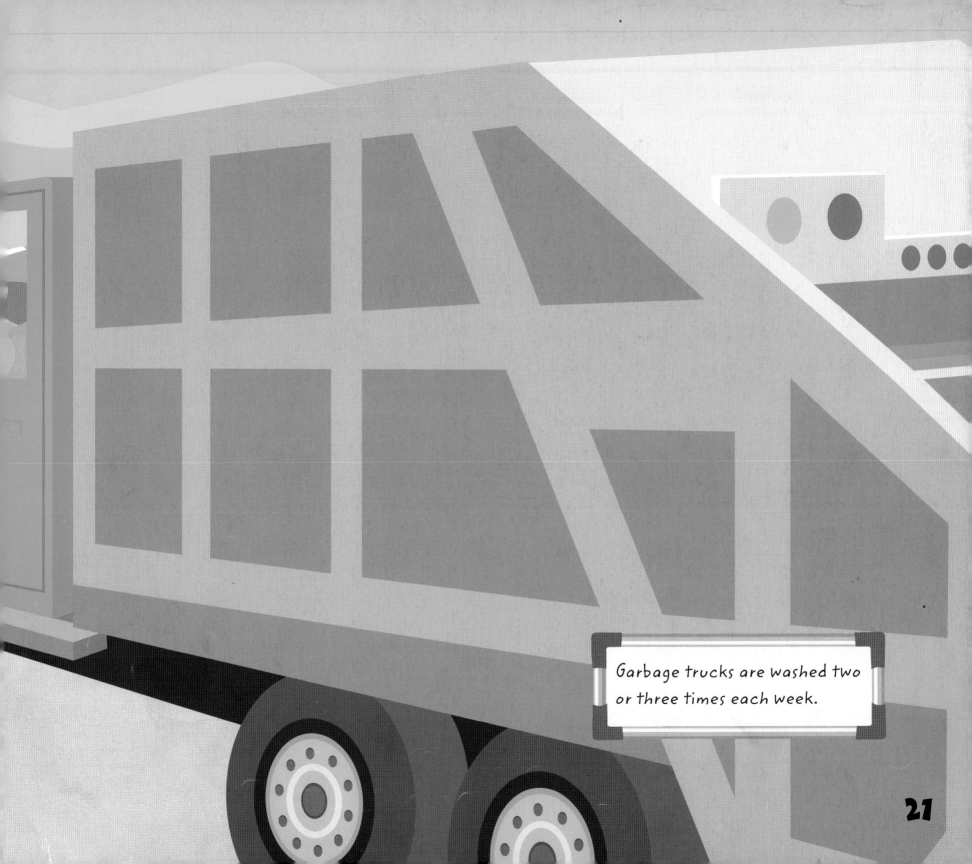

Garbage trucks are washed two or three times each week.

21

GARBAGE TRUCK DIAGRAM

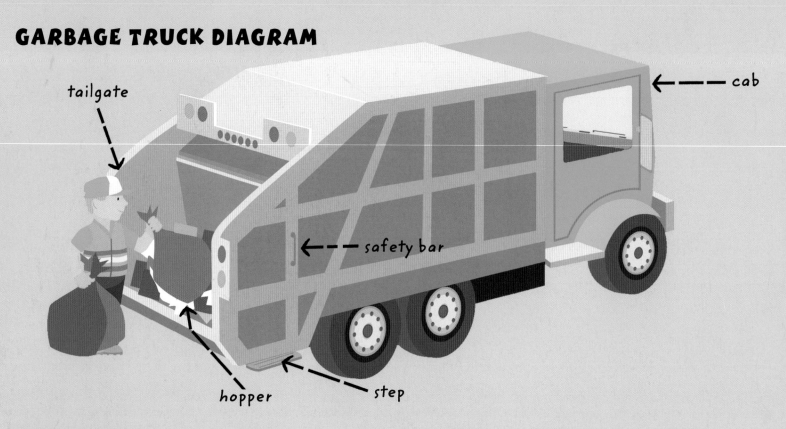

tailgate

cab

safety bar

hopper

step

GLOSSARY

cab—the front of the garbage truck where the driver sits

fluids—liquids in the engine that make it run smoothly

gutter—an area along the edge of a road that helps water drain

incinerator—a place where garbage is burned

landfill—a place where garbage is buried

recycling—the process of using things again instead of throwing them away

FUN FACTS

 Trash collection didn't begin until the 1800s. Before that time, people dumped their garbage in the gutters outside their houses!

 The first garbage trucks were not garbage trucks at all. They were horse-drawn carts! The garbage was hauled to dumps outside of town.

 In big towns, garbage is taken to transfer stations where dump trucks pick it up. The dump trucks drive the garbage to landfills or incinerators far from the city.

 Garbage from a construction site goes to a special place. You can't mix regular trash with construction trash.

 Recycling is not a new idea. The first real recycling program was started in New York City in the 1890s. That's more than 100 years ago!

TO LEARN MORE

At the Library

Deedrick, Tami. *Garbage Collectors.*
Mankato, Minn.: Bridgestone Books, 1998.

Eick, Jean. *Garbage Trucks.* Eden Prairie,
Minn.: Child's World, 1999.

Glaser, Linda. *Stop That Garbage Truck!*
Morton Grove, Ill.: A. Whitman, 1993.

McMullan, Kate. *I Stink!* New York: Joanne
Cotler Books, 2002.

On the Web

FactHound offers a safe, fun way to find Web
sites related to this book. All of the sites on
FactHound have been researched by our staff.
www.facthound.com

1. Visit the FactHound home page.

2. Enter a search word
related to this book,
or type in this special
code: 1404806156.

3. Click on the FETCH IT button.

Your trusty FactHound will fetch the best
Web sites for you!

BOOKS IN THIS SERIES

- I Drive an Ambulance
- I Drive a Bulldozer
- I Drive a Dump Truck
- I Drive a Garbage Truck
- I Drive a Semitruck
- I Drive a Snowplow

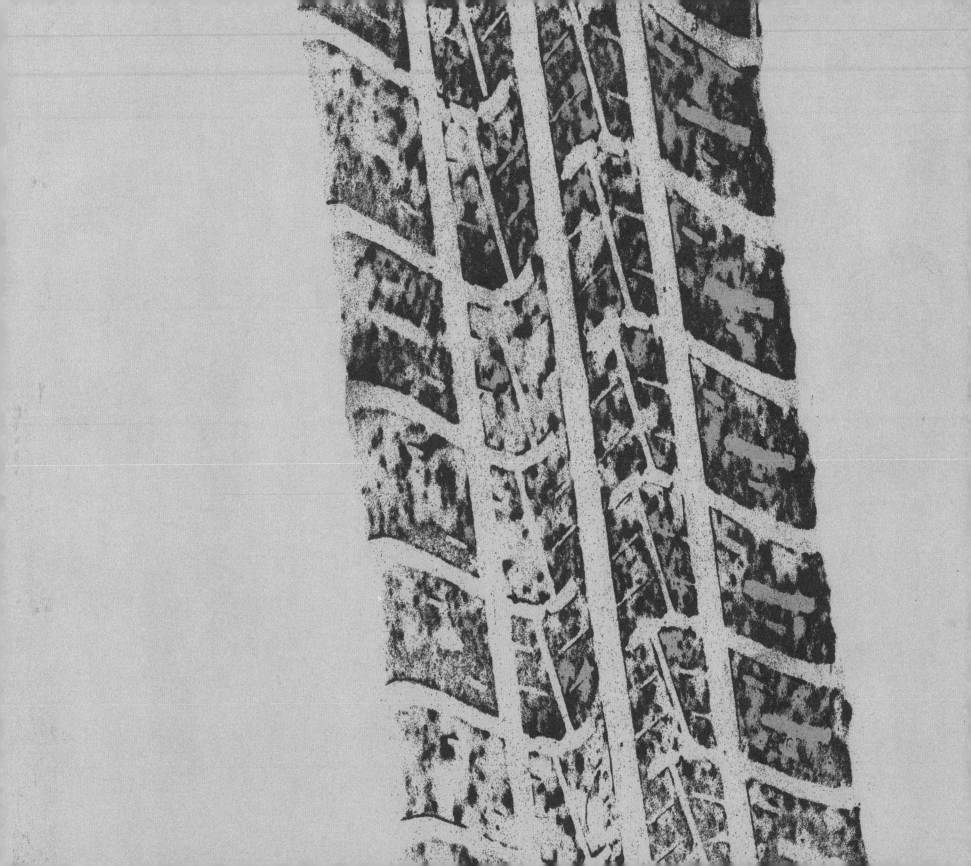